12 THINGS TO KNOW ABOUT
CLIMATE CHANGE

by Jamie Kallio

12 STORY LIBRARY

www.12StoryLibrary.com

12-Story Library is an imprint of Peterson Publishing Company and Press Room Editions.

Produced for 12-Story Library by Red Line Editorial

Photographs ©: Yvonne Pijnenburg-Schonewille/Shutterstock Images, cover, 1 Eugene Hoshiko/AP Images, 4; Mel Evans/AP Images, 5; Artens/Shutterstock Images, 6; kodda/Thinkstock, 7; KenRinger/Thinkstock, 8; Ungnoi Lookjeab/Shutterstock Images, 9, 28; Smileus/Thinkstock, 10; ssuaphotos/Shutterstock Images, 11; rthoma/Shutterstock Images, 12; oticki/Thinkstock, 13; Toa55/Thinkstock, 14; Fedorov Oleksiy/Shutterstock Images, 15; Sergey Rusakov/Thinkstock, 16; La Nau de Fotografia/Shutterstock Images, 17, 29; ChrisDoDutch/Thinkstock, 19; R. Vickers/Shutterstock Images, 20; Brennan Linsley/AP Images, 21; Abd Raouf/AP Images, 22; sprokop/Thinkstock, 23; Whytock/Shutterstock Images, 24; shane partridge/Thinkstock, 25; sunsetman/Shutterstock Images, 26; sigurcamp/Thinkstock, 27

ISBN
978-1-63235-028-2 (hardcover)
978-1-63235-088-6 (paperback)
978-1-62143-069-8 (hosted ebook)

Library of Congress Control Number: 2014946807

Printed in the United States of America
Mankato, MN
October, 2014

Go beyond the book. Get free, up-to-date content on this topic at 12StoryLibrary.com.

TABLE OF CONTENTS

THE EARTH IS WARMING UP

Scientists called climatologists watch and record Earth's temperature. They have found the earth's average temperature is increasing. Earth's climate has always changed naturally over long periods of time. This type of long-term change is called climate change. It is normal for the earth's temperature to fluctuate. However, during the last 150 years, temperatures have risen more rapidly than ever before. Climatologists say that human activity contributes to this change.

The earth's average temperature is normally 59°F (15°C). During the twentieth century, the global temperature increased between 0.7°F and 1.5°F (0.45°C and 0.6°C). The Intergovernmental Panel on Climate Change (IPCC) predicts Earth

Climate scientists from around the world met to discuss climate change in Yokohama, Japan, in 2014.

Climate change can increase the chances of severe weather, including flooding.

could be 2 to 10 degrees warmer in 100 years.

Even a change of just one degree can have disastrous results. As the earth gets hotter, glaciers melt and ocean levels rise. Entire ecosystems are affected. Human lives and whole communities may be endangered. Coastal areas where severe flooding is possible are at risk. Global warming has been blamed for the increase in violent changes in weather.

Most scientists agree steps must be taken to slow global warming. Climate change will impact the earth's natural environment and human population. Most of these impacts will be negative.

2050

The year scientists predict more than 1 million of Earth's plants and animals face extinction if global warming is not slowed.

- Scientific evidence shows human activity is a major cause of global warming.
- Global warming may lead to flooding of coastal areas and extreme weather changes.

5

SOME SCIENTISTS QUESTION CLIMATE CHANGE

Nearly all scientists agree the global temperature is rising. Some, however, do not believe humans are causing global warming and climate change. These people, including some scientists, are called climate change skeptics.

Climate change skeptics argue climatology is still a fairly new science. Global weather patterns are complicated. Scientists are not able to make definite conclusions. Skeptics are not convinced human

Climate change skeptics are not convinced human activity, such as driving, contributes to climate change.

activity is to blame. Earth has been through climate changes before, including ice ages and warming periods. Natural disasters, such as volcanic eruptions, have also changed Earth's climate.

Climate change skeptics point out that Earth has always had cycles of climate change. They say the climate is too complex and powerful. Human actions cannot damage it significantly. Without more research, scientists can only guess

at the future. Skeptics believe more studies are needed before humans take action.

200
Years worth of coal that is located in the United States.

- Most scientists agree that the global temperature is rising.
- People who do not believe humans contribute to global warming are called skeptics.
- Earth has been through climate changes before.

A coal excavator strips coal from a hillside.

GREENHOUSE GASES TRAP HEAT

Increased levels of certain gases in Earth's atmosphere can cause significant changes in climate. These gases, called greenhouse gases, trap heat from the sun. This raises the global temperature of the air and oceans. Currently, Earth's average temperature is around 59°F (14.0°C). Without greenhouse gases, the planet would be a chilly 0°F (-18°C). However, increased levels of greenhouse gases can cause the earth to warm too much.

Human activity releases greenhouse gases into the atmosphere. Energy production and transportation are two big sources of greenhouse gases. Greenhouse gases include carbon dioxide, methane, nitrous oxide, and synthetic gases called chlorofluorocarbons (CFCs). All greenhouse gases trap heat. This warms the earth's surface and leads to changes in the climate.

32
Percentage of US greenhouse gas emissions from electricity generation, the largest US emissions source.

- The United States emits more greenhouse gases than any other country.
- A proper balance of greenhouse gases helps keep the earth's temperature stable.
- Human activity releases greenhouse gases into the atmosphere.

Airplane exhaust releases greenhouse gases.

Smokestacks like these release greenhouse gases into the atmosphere.

4

BURNING FOSSIL FUELS CONTRIBUTES TO CLIMATE CHANGE

Scientists have discovered a dramatic increase of carbon dioxide, or CO_2, levels in Earth's atmosphere. More of this greenhouse gas in the atmosphere causes more heat to be trapped. The heat raises the global average temperature. This leads to changes in Earth's climate. Most scientists think the high levels of CO_2 come from humans' burning of fossil fuels.

Fossil fuels are energy sources found in the earth. Oil, natural gas,

CARBON SINKS

The earth removes CO_2 from the air naturally. To do so, it uses something scientists call a carbon sink. Trees and oceans are carbon sinks because they absorb carbon dioxide. Without carbon sinks, the effects of human-caused climate change would be much worse.

Trees absorb extra carbon dioxide from the atmosphere.

200
Years that CO_2 can last in the atmosphere.

- Scientists have discovered a dramatic increase of CO_2 levels in Earth's atmosphere.
- Most scientists think the high levels of CO_2 that cause climate change come from humans' burning of fossil fuels.
- Humans use fossil fuels for energy and to power machines.
- During the last 150 years, fossil fuel emissions have increased.

and coal are all fossil fuels. These energy sources were formed millions of years ago. During the last 150

THINK ABOUT IT

What is the main idea of these two pages? List at least three pieces of evidence that support your choice.

years, fossil fuel emissions have increased. Humans use fossil fuels for energy and to power machines. Burning fossil fuels releases CO_2 into the atmosphere. The increased levels of greenhouse gases trap a greater amount of heat. This causes the earth to warm and the climate to change.

Car exhaust contains harmful greenhouse gases.

5

FARMING CONTRIBUTES TO CLIMATE CHANGE

Before the use of fossil fuels for energy, farming was a common occupation. Farmers used only a small amount of land. They raised livestock in small numbers. About 150 years ago, fossil fuels started powering farm machinery. With the help of these machines, large pieces of land are used for agriculture.

Cattle in feed lots similar to this one produce methane.

Fertilizers for crops can contribute to global warming.

In 2007, land used for growing crops and raising livestock took up 40 to 50 percent of the earth's land. The use of fertilizer on soil produces large amounts of nitrous oxide. Livestock produce enormous amounts of methane gas in their manure. Both nitrous oxide and methane are powerful greenhouse gases. Nitrous oxide is 300 times more powerful than CO_2 as a greenhouse gas, while methane is 20 times more powerful. They contribute to higher concentrations of greenhouse gases in the atmosphere. Modern farming practices add greatly to global warming.

30
Percentage of Earth's land used by livestock.

- Nearly half the earth's total land is used for farming.
- Methane and nitrous oxide are powerful greenhouse gases.
- Greenhouse gas emissions from farming contribute to climate change.

COW POWER

The methane in cow droppings is a plentiful source of renewable energy. The manure one cow produces daily can light two 100-watt light bulbs for 24 hours!

DEFORESTATION CHANGES CLIMATE

All over the world, forests are being cut down at rapid rates. This is known as deforestation. Since 1950, 30 million acres (12 million ha) of trees have been cut down each year. This equals about 36 football fields per minute. All plants absorb carbon dioxide, but trees do it best. They help keep the earth's temperature consistent.

Changes made to Earth's landscapes, natural or man-made, play a role in climate change. Some deforestation happens naturally, such as through wildfires. However, farmers cut down trees for land on which to plant crops or raise livestock. The logging industry cuts down many more trees than the earth would lose naturally. Forests are also cut down to make way for urban sprawl.

Deforestation causes many negative changes to Earth's ecosystems. Trees hold soil in place and protect groundwater. They provide food and shelter for other plants and animals. Without the trees

Some deforestation is caused by wildfire.

to protect moist forest soils, the sun dries them out. In time, former forests become barren deserts. Trees also return water vapor back into the atmosphere. Without enough trees on Earth, there will be less rain and higher temperatures. There may be more severe weather, such as drought and heat waves, in many regions.

1.6 billion
Number of people who rely on forests for shelter, water, and food.

- Forests are cut down to provide land for grazing, farming, and homes for people.
- Trees absorb carbon dioxide and release water vapor into the atmosphere.
- Deforestation leads to higher temperatures, less rain, and other severe weather.

One example of how deforestation affects the landscape

THE WORLD'S SEA LEVELS ARE RISING

During the twentieth century, scientists found sea levels increased by 6 to 8 inches (15 to 20 cm). If greenhouse gases continue to be emitted at current levels, sea levels could rise 2 feet (.6 m) by the year 2100. This would displace around 60 million people.

Melting glaciers are one reason sea levels are rising. A glacier is a large sheet of snow and ice. Glaciers move slowly down a slope, valley, or over a wide area of land. Scientific reports show that glaciers are melting more quickly now than they have in the past 250 years. Scientists cite global warming as the cause.

To exist, glaciers need certain climate conditions. Most are found in cold, high places such as mountains or in the Polar Regions. As the earth warms, glaciers melt. The runoff flows into the oceans, causing sea levels to rise. Melting ice sheets cause the same problem. The largest ice sheet in the

When chunks of ice fall off glaciers, it is called calving.

POLAR BEARS IN PERIL

Climate change threatens polar bears. Because of shrinking Arctic ice, the bears have a harder time hunting. Scientists predict that two-thirds of the world's remaining 20,000 polar bears will be gone by 2050.

This polar bear navigates ice floating in open water.

temperature rises. When water gets warmer, it expands and takes up more space. More water in the oceans would cover more land, causing floods. Floods threaten coastal cities. In some cases, they can completely submerge low-lying land.

world is the Antarctic ice sheet. The second largest is the Greenland ice sheet. It covers around 80 percent of Greenland's surface. If the Greenland ice sheet completely melted, sea levels would rise by 23 feet (7 m). That would be enough to submerge the cities of London, England, and Los Angeles, California.

Warming global temperatures also cause sea levels to rise. The oceans absorb approximately 80 percent of the extra heat as Earth's

15

Percentage of man-made carbon releases that are absorbed by the Southern Ocean yearly in Antarctica.

- As oceans absorb more carbon dioxide, their water becomes more acidic, destroying the shells of sea life.
- Melting glaciers are one reason sea levels are rising.
- Melting ice sheets add to rising sea levels.

COUNTRIES ARE ADAPTING TO CLIMATE CHANGE

The effects of climate change are already being felt the world over. Failure to adapt puts people all over the world at risk. Some countries are investing in new technologies to adapt to climate change.

With rising sea levels, 300 million people are threatened by coastal flooding. The Netherlands is a country where 60 percent of people live below sea level. It has long dealt

The Eastern Scheldt Storm Surge Barrier protects the Netherlands from the North Sea.

100 million

Number of people scientists predict will be affected by annual coastal flooding by 2080.

- Humans are finding ways to adapt to climate change.
- 300 million people are currently threatened by coastal flooding.
- To deal with flooding, the Netherlands built the complex Delta Works system.

OTHER CITIES PREPARE

Cities such as London, England, and St. Petersburg, Russia, have their own moveable storm barriers. Venice, Italy, is working on a similar barrier. These are examples of humans planning for future climate change.

with flooding from the North Sea. In 1953, the North Sea rose over the dikes of Zeeland province and killed more than 1,800 people. Between 1950 and 1997, the Dutch built the Delta Works to stop such a disaster from happening again.

The Delta Works is a network of dikes and 65 gates. It spans the southwest side of the country. The greatest feature of the Delta Works is the Eastern Scheldt Storm Surge Barrier. The barrier is a 5-mile (8-km) dam with enormous gates. The gates can be raised to make the dam watertight. The Delta Works was built to protect the Netherlands for 200 years.

THE ARCTIC IS WARMING FASTER THAN OTHER REGIONS

Typically, the Arctic has a harsh, cold climate and treeless plains called tundra. Beneath the tundra is permafrost, or permanently frozen rock or soil. Scientists have found that the Arctic's permafrost is melting. Satellite data shows Arctic sea ice has shrunk in every month since 1979.

The Arctic region is found in the northernmost part of the earth. It contains the Arctic Ocean and parts of eight countries. Humans have lived in the Arctic for thousands of

Permafrost is not always covered in snow.

4 million

Number of people who live in the Arctic region.

- Melting permafrost threatens the way of life for people who live in the Arctic.
- Arctic ice has melted away every month for 35 years.
- Warmer temperatures in the Arctic threaten animals, including caribou, whales, and seals.

years. They have adapted their way of life around the climate. Warmer temperatures and less ice have forced people to use boats instead of dog sleds or snowmobiles. Many Arctic people rely on whales, seals, caribou, and fish for food. Climate change threatens their food supplies and livelihoods.

THINK ABOUT IT

What are some ways native people in the Arctic are affected by climate change? Use information from these pages and another source to support your answer.

An Inuit man uses a boat to navigate the Arctic waters.

CLIMATE CHANGE COULD CAUSE EXTREME WEATHER

Scientists believe climate changes are responsible for changing weather patterns. Some of these changed patterns are extreme. Extreme weather includes heat waves, droughts, flooding, blizzards, and colder-than-normal winters. All over the world, extreme weather events and patterns are occurring more often. Scientists predict extreme weather events such as hurricanes, storms, and floods are likely to get worse as global temperatures rise.

Global warming has many effects on precipitation. Too much precipitation can cause flooding. In 2007, Sudan experienced flash floods that affected 500,000 people. That same year, areas of the United Kingdom also experienced

Men struggle to keep their vehicles afloat during the Sudan floods in 2007.

major flooding. The floods were the result of the highest amount of monthly rainfall ever recorded.

Hurricanes are strong tropical storms. When they reach land, heavy rain, strong winds, and large waves can damage buildings, trees, and cars. In 2004 and 2005, Earth experienced 4 out of the 10 most extreme Atlantic hurricanes ever recorded. They caused severe damage to the coastlands along the Gulf of Mexico. The increase in tropical storm activity was related to increased temperatures of sea surfaces.

81 billion
Dollars of damage hurricanes caused along the Gulf Coast in 2005.

- Scientists believe climate change is responsible for extreme weather patterns.
- Extreme weather is occurring more frequently all over the world.
- The IPCC stated that the increase in tropical storm activity was related to increased temperatures of sea surfaces.

CLIMATE VS. WEATHER

Is it cloudy? Sunny? Rainy? These are all weather questions. Weather is the way the atmosphere behaves from day to day. Climate describes the long-term pattern of weather in a certain area. For example, the climate of Arizona is warm with low humidity. Weather can be predicted, but it changes every day. Climate stays the same day to day.

Cacti thrive in the hot, dry Arizona climate.

CLIMATE CHANGE ALTERS ECOSYSTEMS

Climate change is greatly harming whole ecosystems. Many plants and animals struggle to adapt to new weather patterns. Some have moved farther north to cooler climates or into deeper waters. Many animals have to change their behaviors. For example, some birds are breeding and migrating earlier as spring arrives sooner in many regions.

The plants and animals that cannot adapt or move are in danger of becoming extinct. Certain plants and flowers rely on insects to spread their pollen. If these plants bloom sooner than insects become active, they are unable to multiply. If certain plants decrease in number dramatically or die out completely, animal species that depend on them

Climate change may cause birds to alter their migration patterns.

These koalas' habitat may be threatened by climate change.

50

Percentage of managed honeybee colonies in the United States that have been lost over the past 10 years.

- Whole ecosystems are affected by climate change.
- Changes in seasons are causing migratory animals to travel sooner, which may disrupt food and habitat availability.

will also suffer. For example, koala bears mainly live off eucalyptus leaves. Eucalyptus trees require cool climates to grow, but heat waves and droughts are threatening them. If the number of eucalyptus trees starts to decline, so will the number of koala bears. To save thousands of species, scientists must discover ways to considerably reduce greenhouse gases.

HUMANS CAN MAKE A DIFFERENCE

The global climate is a complex topic. Data about weather patterns change constantly. There is much information to study. Scientists can agree, however, that the earth is warming.

There are things everyone can do to reduce the effects of global warming. Even small changes can make a difference. *Reduce, reuse, recycle* is a phrase that can help people remember that their actions affect the earth. Driving a car, using electricity from fossil fuels to light homes, and throwing away garbage all produce greenhouse gases. People can reduce these emissions by driving their cars less, using less power, and recycling. Some

Cities are making it easier for people to recycle.

people compost their garbage, which lessens the amount that ends up in landfills.

Governments across the world are exploring other ways to help limit the damage caused by global warming. The United States is developing ways to use more renewable energy sources instead of fossil fuels. New and old buildings can save energy by insulating their walls. They can also add solar panels to retain heat from the sun. Cutting back on deforestation and planting more trees will absorb more CO_2 from the atmosphere. These strategies can go a long way in slowing down climate change.

Wind power is one example of renewable energy.

1970
Year the United States Environmental Protection Agency was created to enforce national pollution-control standards.

- Scientists agree that the world is warming.
- *Reduce, reuse, recycle* is a phrase to help people make a difference in slowing climate change.
- Governments are working to develop renewable energy.
- Planting more trees will help absorb more CO_2.

THINK ABOUT IT

Create a plan for how your class will help reduce the effects of climate change. Use the ideas on these pages and from one other source to write your plan. Include at least three actions your class can take.

FACT SHEET

- Throughout time, Earth has undergone variations in climate, such as ice ages and warming periods. However, most scientists believe human activity is largely responsible for recent climate change.

- Fossil fuels, which humans rely on for energy, create greenhouse gases such as carbon dioxide, methane, and nitrous oxide. Too high of a concentration of these gases in Earth's atmosphere leads to an increase in global warming. Global warming is the increase in the earth's overall temperature, specifically outside the normal temperature variations.

- Trees are important absorbers of carbon dioxide, a greenhouse gas. Old-growth tropical rain forests are Earth's most diverse ecosystems. However, 30 million acres (12 million ha) of trees, including those in tropical forests, are cut down each year. Deforestation alters ecosystems, reduces rainfall, and reduces the number of trees that absorb CO_2.

- Arctic sea ice has decreased 14 percent since the 1970s. During the twentieth century, sea levels have risen between 6 to 8 inches (15 to 20 cm). Melting glaciers such as the Greenland ice sheet will contribute to even higher sea levels. If sea levels rise much more, coastal areas are under threat of extreme flooding.

- Scientists blame extreme weather patterns, such as stronger storms and hurricanes, on recent climate change. They predict weather across the globe will become more extreme as the earth continues to warm.

- Rising temperatures and changing lengths of seasons will alter entire ecosystems. Some living things in altered ecosystems will adapt; others will die out and become extinct.

- Climate change skeptics are not sure climate change is caused by human activities. They point out that Earth has experienced extreme natural climate changes before, such as the Toba volcanic explosion.

GLOSSARY

atmosphere
The mass of air that surrounds Earth.

climatologists
Scientists who study climate.

climatology
The study of climates.

compost
A mixture of decaying organic substances used for fertilizing soil.

deforestation
The result of cutting down all the trees in an area.

dikes
Mounds of earth used to prevent water from flooding certain areas.

ecosystem
Everything that exists in a certain environment.

emissions
Harmful substances released by the burning of fossil fuels.

extinction
A situation that occurs when a species no longer exists.

fossil fuel
A fuel that is formed in the earth from dead plants or animals.

precipitation
Water that falls to the ground in the form of rain, snow, or ice.

renewable energy
An energy source, such as the sun, that can never be used up.

synthetic
An unnatural substance.

urban sprawl
Buildings, houses, and stores built in an area around a city that formerly had few people living in it.

water vapor
Water in its gaseous state.

FOR MORE INFORMATION

Books

Arnold, Caroline. *A Warmer World: From Polar Bears to Butterflies, How Climate Change Affects Wildlife.* Watertown, MA: Charlesbridge, 2012.

Brezina, Corona. *Climate Change.* New York: Rosen Publishing, 2008.

Shea, Nicole. *Animals and Climate Change.* New York: Gareth Stevens Publishing, 2014.

Woodward, John. *Eyewitness Climate Change.* New York: DK Publishing, 2008.

Websites

Climate Kids: NASA's Eyes on the Earth
www.climatekids.nasa.gov

Global Warming Kids.net
www.globalwarmingkids.net

A Student's Guide to Global Climate Change
www.epa.gov/climatechange/kids

INDEX

About the Author

Jamie Kallio is a youth services librarian in the south suburbs of Chicago. She received an MFA in writing for children and young adults from Hamline University in Minnesota and is the author of several nonfiction books for children.

READ MORE FROM 12-STORY LIBRARY

Every 12-Story Library book is available in many formats, including Amazon Kindle and Apple iBooks. For more information, visit your device's store or 12StoryLibrary.com.